CW00419414

Let's Write
Hammersmith and Fulham
2023

Let's Write Hammersmith and Fulham 2023 was a project born from the Hammersmith and Fulham Writers' Festival.

This project was a collaboration between a number of local organisations and individuals which resulted in a range of activities and events being successfully delivered to over a hundred young people aged 7 to 12 across the borough:

Write-London and Shepherds Bush Library ran a day of creative workshops at Old Oak Primary School

Write-London held a six week after-school writing group at SEACC (Sands End Arts & Community Centre) in partnership with them and SEAPIA (Sands End Associated Projects in Action)

Tideway funded a 3-day half-term creative writing project at SEACC delivered by Write-London

As part of the 2023 Hammersmith and Fulham Writers' Festival, Shepherds Bush Library hosted a day of creative events for children with workshops delivered by Kamapala Chukwuka, Richard Trautmann and Tom Mallender. In addition to this work, Tom Mallender, Mandy Charles and Joyce Osei delivered a day of workshops for the pupils of Langford Primary School hosted by SEACC

An evening of poetry and short story readings was hosted in September by SEACC in partnership with Tideway, SEAPIA and Write-London to celebrate the work done in Sands End as part of Let's Write Hammersmith and Fulham 2023. This work was first published as a solo volume titled *"The Sands End Young People's Anthology 2023"*. The work within that volume has been included in this anthology to fully reflect and showcase all the work the young people of Hammersmith and Fulham created during 2023.
A showcase event is planned for January 2024 along with the first Let's Write Hammersmith and Fulham Awards to reward the young writers who took part in this project.

Work is underway to expand upon the achievements of 2023 and to make Let's Write Hammersmith and Fulham 2024 an even greater success. We want to work with more young people in more areas of Hammersmith and Fulham to give them an opportunity to tell and share the stories they want to tell.

The work contained in this anthology is transcribed from the original drafts. Minor spelling corrections have been made but no other editorial changes have been added, thus the work that follows is the authentic voice of the children who created it. Any mistakes in the transcription of the work are totally the fault of Tom Mallender and Naino Masindet.

Thanks

Let's Write Hammersmith and Fulham 2023 was a true collaboration and without the input of many people it would never have happened.

Special thanks must go to Sharon Tomlin for making many of the initial introductions between Write-London and the various partners who helped deliver this project.

Thanks also goes to Rasheda Malcolm for founding and directing the Hammersmith and Fulham Writers' Festival which was the spark for Let's Write Hammersmith and Fulham.

I would like to thank all the artists who delivered workshops and helped in the facilitation of the project: Joyce Osei, Kamapala Chukwuka, Naino Masindet and Richard Trautmann. Their work made this project possible.

Many local organisations and individuals gave their time, premises and support to this project which made it possible. Please check the partner details to see the wonderful work these organisations do but special thanks to Julie Cavanagh, Christopher Newport, John Sage, Shanice Phillips, Old Oak Primary School & Langford Primary School.

A final thanks must be given to Mandy Charles who fulfilled so many roles during this project it can't be overstated how much is owed to her hard work.

Tom Mallender (November 2023)

Project Partners

Write-London

Write-London is a community-based literature and art project working with people to create poems and other short form writings, along with art works that reflect upon those writings.

Listening to participants is at the very core of everything that Write-London does. Every workshop, reading, exhibition and publication is a collaboration between the artists facilitating the work and the participant artists creating the work.

Write-London exists to facilitate in people telling the stories that they want to tell.

SEACC

Sands End Arts & Community Centre is extremely proud to have been part of The Sands End Young People's Anthology.

All those who contributed to the book should be extremely pleased with what they have achieved – this book is testament to their hard work and we hope it serves as platform for them to explore other creative outlets in the future.

SEAPIA

SEAPIA provides an inclusive, good quality, affordable, safe, and enriching environment for all C&YP aged 4-13 in the local area of Sands End.

We have a high local profile and are recognised for our activities within the community.

We provide activities that empower C&YP to develop as individuals and enjoy new challenges through social action.

Our service is accessible after school and during school holidays 50 weeks of the year. During school holidays we provide up to 3 off-site trips per week.

As well as our open access service we provide a self-funded childcare facility which meets a specific need in the Sands End area.

We work in partnership with local schools and other organisations and make great efforts to ensure we are meeting the needs of C&YP and their families.

Tideway

Tideway is proud to support the creative writing programme at the Sands End Arts and Community Centre – this book really shows how writing can give young people a new outlet for their creativity, helping them to feel good as well as creating something exciting. Our project is cleaning up the River Thames for future generations and the work showcased here demonstrates why SEACC, the biggest investment in our programme to create a community legacy, can play its own vital role in supporting future generations. Well done to all the young people who contributed to this book and happy reading!

Shepherds Bush Library

H&F Libraries are situated in the heart of a culturally diverse London borough, and we were delighted to support this initiative. We are passionate about creative writing which enables children to express themselves and explore their feelings through the power of words. Creative writing activities support educational and wellbeing needs. It was lovely to see the children using their imagination, showing empathy, and empowering themselves with words during our workshops in partnership with local schools.

- **Mandy Charles (Service Delivery Manager)**

Let's Write
Hammersmith and Fulham
2023

Contents

(Part One)

(Part Two)

Part One

The majority of these short stories and poems were created during a morning of creative writing with Year Three (7-8 years old) at Old Oak Primary School and at SEACC (Sands End Arts & Community Centre) with Year Three from Langford Primary School.

In addition to the work created during these sessions, more young writers aged between 6 and 11 took part in the project with a day of creative writing activities hosted at Shepherds Bush Library.

McDonald's

I eat chips, chips, chips and more chips. I really want to drink the Grimace Shake because people say it tastes good. I like to eat ice cream.

by Freeman

The Boy with The Majestic Prime

Once upon a time there lived a wealthy boy named Troll. His dad was a billionaire and one time they ran out of milk. So the boy swiftly rushed towards Sainsbury's. He grabbed the milk and hastily ran to his dad. His dad gave him a couple thousand pounds to buy KSI Prime. He swiftly ran with his overjoyed face to the shop. He didn't find the Prime but he did find a rainbow Prime and when he returned home he drank the Prime. His mouth was dripping with saliva and entered a different galaxy.

by Harry

1

One day in a library there was a girl called Caroline, and she was playfully reading until... *flicker* *flicker* went the lights. Slowly she raised her head, realising she would be doomed for a lifetime. Her one and only nightmare had come true! A stiff doll stood on top of a green table with the sharpest knife ever: the carving knife. The doll wore a baby frock with a bonnet. She had her left eye flickering constantly, whilst her right stood still. NO MOVEMENT. Caroline tried to back off/back away, but then her back hit the glass, so she thought, "This is it. No escape now, Caroline." It sounded like a creepy nursery rhyme repeating[...]. Sweat came out of her pores and down her face, and it fell. It was as quiet as water (a drop) touching the ground.

by Mercy

McDonald's is a fast food restaurant which originally started in the United States of America. Most people go to McDonald's all around the world and it is one of the most popular fast food restaurants around the globe. It is estimated that around 2 billion people go to McDonald's every day. A few characters appear in the world of McDonald's such as Ronald McDonald, Grimace and many more characters appear. One of the most famous drinks around the world in McDonald's is Cola and the All New GRIMACE SHAKE! It is very viral across the world and it is found everywhere. McDonald's is very good. McDonald's is very good. McDonald's is really...

MALFUNCTION

by Otto

In Westfield I go to the toy shop and buy things. In Westfield I go to the Lego shop and look at the Lego and sometimes buy Lego. In Westfield I go to John Lewis and buy clothes. In Westfield I hear a lot of noises.

by Idu

Once there was a boy which wanted to become an amazing footballer but after he saw Chelsea lose to Man City he decided to train even harder. Also he wanted to win the World Cup and the Premier League when he becomes a footballer. His goal was to join Man City.

When he became 15 years old his mum allowed him to play for Chelsea.

by Marat

Adventures in London

Once upon a time, there was a girl called Naya and a boy called Adnan. They liked adventures and they wanted to go and then they saw a treasure hunt and wanted to play. They played and they won and they really wanted to go and eat. Soon they helped their dad to clean up the house, they were exhausted from cleaning. After, they went to sleep and they wanted to hear a bedtime story and then they went to sleep. One day they were dreaming of going to a fun day in their dreams. They woke up with no energy and they didn't want to do cleaning.

The End

by Adnan

What if your cat eats dog food and can bark. It pees like a dog and it would chase the neighbour's cat and he goes to the park with a leash and he plays fetch.

by Samba

The Tiger in Gambado

Once there lived a tiger named Roar. Roar loved jumping up and down. His owner was annoyed so she sent Roar to Gambado. Roar started scaring everyone so he could have the place all for himself. One little girl wasn't afraid and she jumped on the tiger's shoulder and for the rest of the day they both were playing on the bumper cars. They lived happily ever after.

by Maya

It Is Fun to Climb

It is fun to climb you can float.
You can climb as high as you can.
You can try.
You can touch the sky.
You are brave.
You can do this.
You can do your best.
You can climb like a monkey.
You can go down slides.
You can be the best you've ever been.

by Nadia

Alison and Keiran on Their Adventures to Clip 'n Climb

Once there lived a beautiful girl called Alison and a mature, friendly boy named Kieran. Alison once woke up with this active feeling that made her keep up awake. Suddenly Kieran woke up and cried, "I... I... h...have this feeling A-Alison..." "Yes Keiran, I know. I have that as well." replied Alison. "Let's just go back to sleep." said mum appearing out of nowhere. "Huh? Mum? What on earth are you doing here?" "Just sayin' that active feeling of yours. I have it too." It was a feeling that made them want to go to Clip 'n Climb.*

*Clip 'n Climb is a climbing spot for children to go get some fun!

To be continued...

*said mum.

by Sidra F

A few years ago there lived two girls. They were called Nialah and Sidra, they loved climbing and another friend of theirs came along that was called Kenza. Soon they went to climb a real enormous mountain and they climbed really high. Suddenly Kenza fell down, we tried to save her but we sadly couldn't save her. We didn't climb for 34 weeks. Next, Nialah told Sidra omg look at this tall wall. They climbed it when they wanted to get done. Suddenly!

To be continued

by Sidra A

Emily and The Magic Cup

Once upon a time there was a little girl named
Emily. She lives right next to Chelsea Creek with
her mom and dad and also with her brother Mike.
One evening, Mike and Emily were playing in their
room. "It's time to go to sleep!" suggested mom.
"Ok mommy!" said Mike and Emily at the same
time. When they both fell asleep they both fell into
a dream. They found themselves in a huge cup!
They flew to Sweden, Finland, Egypt, England,
Ireland and many more fun adventures carried on.
The next morning, Mike and Emily told their mom
and dad about all of the adventures.

The End

by Nusaybah

I would like a dog as a pet because they are fluffy and they do tricks.

***

When I played for my team I scored the winning goal. I felt happy and excited.

by Reggie

I have a pet cat. I want to give her a silly name and name her a cat[...]. Cat likes to play and sleep.

***

What if I played football, run along the pitch and then jumped into the pool. The water splashed out. Then all the people jumped out and landed on the grass.

by Ritaj

Today I am fixing my cat because he is acting like a dog. He is peeing like a dog and chasing the neighbour's cat and eating dog food. He wrecked the house, smashed the vase, I put it in the lab and experimented on him to be a cat but that did not work till lightning struck him and he died.

***

Today I am going to combine football and swimming. I am in the swimming pool-- oh no it is floating help me get it down, let's add weights to it that it's better but it would not move.

***

Today I am playing football for Arsenal and I scored the winning goal for them and won the FA cup and won the Champion's League and the Premier League.

by Abdullahi

What if Your Hamster Wasn't Nocturnal?

Today when I went to my hamster she was awake?
So I went to the vet and they said it was fine?
What?!?! So I went back home and played with her.
But it was weird. So I visited my nephews and
forgot all about the nocturnal stuff, and I also
brought Mini Oreo the hamster with me! She loves
getting attention from my nephews!

***

Today my brother tried doing athletics and
gymnastics at the same time!?!? Wow. But he told
me it wasn't that hard? Well... I kinda believe him.
What? Athletics and gymnastics are quite the same!
He also said that he was on the team called: THE
HUSKIES. It was quite a good name! I love huskies!
Anyway I might try it too!

by Sophia

Today I invented a device that makes it possible to talk to animals. It is a carpet and if you roll it on the floor and place an animal on it, it can talk like a human. I brought 100 cats, 100 horses, 100 dogs and 100 turtles. I rolled the carpet on the floor and placed all the animals on the carpet.

All of a sudden I heard several shouts and screams. I heard, "OH NO WE GOT CAPTURED BY THAT HORRIBLE HUMAN!" I was baffled. "I'm not a horrible human!" I screamed. After I said that there was silence. All the animals stared at me with wonder. "Did she just talk?" asked a horse named Betty. "I think so?" whispered a cat called Emily. "Okay just understand this. The carpet under you is magical." I explained. "AAAA!" they screamed.

Very soon after they screamed I heard a knock. *Oh no it might be my nosy neighbour,* I thought. I quickly rolled the carpet with the animals still in there. I put on loud music to cover the muffled sounds. I opened the door. I was right, it was my nosy neighbour. "I thought I thought I heard some sounds," she said.

***

Today I tried to play swimming and basketball together. It's quite hard to play in a swimming suit. It was sooo fun still. We had to swim underwater to get the ball first and then swim up without the ball falling back and score the goal. I was on Red Tigers team and the other team was Winning Lizards. I scored all the goals today. After the game, everybody voted for me to be the new captain because I also scored the winning goal. The finals are tomorrow and my case of medals is already full! This is the only time my school got into the finals! Oh better go it's time for school!
"Coming, mum!"

by Rameen

If a monkey escaped the zoo, so many zookeepers would try and get the monkey so the monkey would try and run away from the zoo. So the monkey went to the jungle and found lots of monkeys there so he went to the monkeys but the zookeepers found the monkeys so the monkeys ran away from the zookeepers so the other monkeys got captured and the monkey ran across the road. He ran across the park then he found his wife Beyoncé then he got married so him and his wife found an owner.

***

If we combined football and dodgeball we'll have to throw the ball at the goalkeeper.

***

If I scored the winning goal I would try and get to a better team so I can get more money.

by Musab

Jolof

Jolof is a football club in Sands End. There is a lot of people there.

Fun Facts:

Jolof wins a lot of tournaments for example they won one that was 5-0.
They won over one hundred cups!
It is the best team in England!

You will never see an own goal, a open goal miss or even a corner in embarrassing moments!

Jolof hardly loses, they only lose when they are not playing their best but they score every match.

The End

(Jolof is the best)

by Voita

Sainsbury's Shop

Once upon a time a boy called Messi, he loved football. He really wanted to play in a football world cup. His mum said, "when you're 23."

"Mum I'm only 11."

"And?" said mum. "You only need to wait 12 years." exclaimed mum. Then dad walks in.

by Nami

Sainsbury's

One day I go to the Sainsbury's and pay the horse then I go home. Ride on my horse, jump aaaaAAAA

by Zlata

The Adventure at Pineapple Park

Once upon a time there was a girl called Sofia. She was going to Pineapple Park every day after school. She was going to Pineapple Park then she found an Adventures castle! She went in it! People were there, she made so many friends! "Wow I have so many friends!" exclaimed Sofia. Finally she found a treasure chest. Thank you friends, thank you very much for being my friends.

by Aya

Two Friends

Once there were two friends called Ralph and
Vivan. They were playing Fortnite after Ralph's
mom came over to collect Ralph so Vivan begged
for Ralph to stay over so his mum whispered, "Ok."
"Yahoo!" squealed Vivan and Ralph. They slept in
their sleeping bags and had a dream about Vivan
and Ralph playing cricket.

by Vivan

Where I go, asked the jellyfish. I don't know.

by Dylan

Chelsea Harbour

Chelsea Harbour is a busy area with a shiny river. Many people live here. You'll get the luxury houses at the waterfront drive. There's an automatic sliding bronze gate for the carpark. You also get a specially prepared key when you walk in, you'll see all of the mailboxes then you'll make you way to the stairs or elevator. When you get to your floor you'll see polished carpets and walls, powerful doorbells and when you're in you have great monitors. Visit now!

by Rosalie

A Story with a Boy that Dreams Come True

Once there was 1 kid. He had 1 sister that is older. The younger brother's name was Alex, his sister was Daisy. After when it was the morning they decided to go to Fulham Broadway. After they bought snacks like milk for cereal and bought ice lollies. When they went to their house it was bed time. After he went to bed he wished to get a golden cup and have a cupcake. Suddenly he was in his wish. He was very scared after he went to explore.

Suddenly he saw a golden cup and cupcake and he was in the beach but when he went to get the golden cup it was only £2, he was stunned. He liked to get a cupcake, he had £4 left. The cupcake was £1 so he ate the cake. After he went out of his dream he had a cupcake and a golden cup. He told his sister and she was amazed. "How did you get that?" "It was my dream! So we can wish anything!!!" "Let's wish to be rich!"

The End

by Damontae

A Fun Time at South Park

One day I was wandering around in South Park
with my friends. When we found a clear space we
set down a picnic. Next we set down two goals to
play football and we made a huge football
tournament and whoever won could pick 5 people
to go to a huge party. And whoever lost would still
have a fun time there. There were 4 teams which
were the Huge Ice Blocks, the Burning Wolves, the
Fantastic Ballers and the Ferocious Bears.

When it started it was the Fantastic Ballers and the
Huge Ice Blocks. At the end it was 2-1 for the
Fantastic Ballers. Then the Burning Wolves were
against the Ferocious Bears and it was 0-0 at the
end. The finals were intense and it was 5-5 and they
both had a fun party while the others had a fun
little picnic.

by Ralph

Captain to Go to Westfield

One time there was a captain that met a boy named Greg Hoseley and another boy named Bahman, they went to Westfield. "I love Westfield," exclaimed Bahman. They met another boy named Keyan. They became best friends[...]. "Let's go to Kidzania!" shouted Greg. "Yes, let's go!" yelled Bahman.

"Adventures are fun when friends are around," whispered everyone. "It sure is," gasped Bahman.

Friends always come back.
Fun is not over yet.
It's sure not over.
It's time to go home.
"Bye everyone," gulped Bahman.
Adventure is over.

The End

By Keyan

My cat thinks it's a dog because it will bark and play fetch and plays with a ball and my cat chews bones and runs fast and chases other dogs and goes round in circles.

***

In gymnastics I compete with my teammates and I sometimes win a gold medal and I feel proud. When I'm on stage I feel nervous and happy at the same time.

by Sumaiyah

If I had a pet I will choose a cat because it is cute and it chews my socks. And I will name it Lily the cat. I will give my cat cat food and it will step in my house.

***

If I was playing gymnastics and I was in a competition on the beam and I won I will be over the moon and if I failed I will be so sad. If I was doing a handstand competition and I won I will get a gold medal and I will do the splits at the end and I will feel happy and nervous. Today I was doing swimming and gymnastics with my friends Sumaiyah, Shylie and me and Ella. Bye now.

by Suraiyah

What if... you had a cat and when you were cooking it jumped at you and burnt you so badly you went to the hospital and broke your leg and arm.

***

I am in a swimming team in the Olympics for a gold medal and I won. Everybody was so happy and I got to be the captain and I was the best captain.

by Intisar

If I had a pet it would probably be a chimpanzee and they're really naughty and would probably break something and it's really hard to find food for the chimpanzees.

***

If I was playing football and I was in Al-Nassr and I won the World Cup I would do a celebration and thank my grandma and I will feel proud.

by Walid

27

What if you don't have a pet what animal would you like as your pet?

If I had a pet I would like a lion. There would be no room in my bedroom.

***

I would like to play for Manchester United in the FA Cup Final and win and I would like to play in the Champion's League and win and I will be excited.

by Jahnari

What if you have a device that makes it possible to talk to a monkey?
I would talk to my friend. Monkey likes to climb, swing on trees.

***

When I play for my team I scored the winning goal. I felt happy.

by Ali

What if you invent a device that makes it possible to talk to animals?

When I say good morning to the pandas I would say..... could I cuddle you then I would cuddle them. I would stay with them and give them bamboo and leaves. I would ask animal doctors to translate to speak to pandas. I would ask to name them names.

***

My friend called Ella really wanted to do both of my sports: gymnastics and swimming. When it was my big concert my friend joined in as well, my coach was Marikk[...]. When we did our swimming concert, Ella thought when she came out of the swimming pool she thought that we were in a gymnastics concert. I said to Ella, "Are you out of your mind this is not the gymnastics concert, us and the people and our coaches have to drive to get there. What a silly," I said. Then we went to the Olympics station to perform. I did 10 splits, 10 backflips and guess what? All our team got first place and we did it with teamwork.

by Shylie

What if you don't have a pet, what animal would you like as your pet?

Pitbull because they're very strong and they look cool and I'll take a walk with my pitbull.

***

So when you are swimming you're actually playing football so when you kick the ball you can't feel the ball and the goal is floating and the ball is like flat so you have to use your head so when the ball is coming to you you have to dive in to the ball with your head and if you are a goalie you have to float to the ball with your head or with your hand.

by Aaqib

What I Do at Football Club

Fulham United is a football club. What I do there is I play with my friends and they come to my club. I like going there because football is my favourite sport. I play up front and my friend plays midfield. He sometimes sets me up so I can score. They also play on my team and on my team I have a great goalkeeper, he never puts an open goal or he never does an own goal, that's why he is a great goalkeeper. I also have an amazing defender, he always saves a goal. He can also score from the halfway line.

by Izet

What to Play in Adventure

In Adventure you can play games such as football and basketball. Adventure is right next to Langford and when you go to Adventure you might be happy because it has lots of activities such as football and dodgeball. Also in Adventure you can play ping-pong[...].

by Kaylen

What If You Don't Have a Pet

If I had a pet it will be called Blaze. It will be a tarantula. He will be in a cage, I would feed him a fly every day. If I let if go it will scare somebody.

by Zain

The Two Best Friends

One day when Adelaide was at her gymnastics she found a girl called Alice. Her and Adelaide immediately became friends for they both bonded over much. After gymnastics the two new friends played adventures at the South Park. They loved exploring through the bushes. Although it was time to go after long. Alice and Adelaide still are great friends.

Then they were doing one of their adventures, they got surrounded by snakes! So they quickly hopped on helicopters and flew to Australia. There they fell asleep upside down with the bats. After they smushed leaves to get clean water and ate some carrots they found on a hill but it was hard to get the carrots for the mountain was very steep so they asked a goat to take them up in exchange for some of the carrots. They found the goat but they had to cross a lava pit so they swung across vines to rescue the goat and get the carrots. Wait till next time to see what adventures happen next!

by Adelaide

Another Again

Once at South Park there was a lost cat that didn't like having fur. The cat was never born because one day she just appeared out of nowhere!

Then one day another cat came by and also didn't have any owner. Then the cat saw the other cat and just remembered that exactly the same thing has happened before. But then the other cat went to her and asked her name. She didn't really know what to say so she said her nickname. So she said that her name was Allie. Then the other cat said her name. The other cat said that her name was Lilly.

Lilly followed Allie everywhere but then one day Allie noticed that but Lilly kept doing it, it got a bit nerve-racking for Allie. So one day Allie stood up for herself and said, "Stop following me Lilly." So then Lilly stopped doing that and Allie found herself a new friend.

by Alisa

A Magic Place

One day, a girl called Rima was eating her special breakfast because... it was her birthday. Normally each year her parents bring her to Fulham library and can get as many books as she could but this year it was different.

Normally she recognised a path to the library. "What's this place?" asked Rima to her parents. SURPRISE! The room was all dark with loads of bright lights, the walls were formed differently. It was a climbing place. Rima was really shy, she doesn't know how to climb.

Just then, a woman with beautiful dark hair with wide eyes came straight to the family. "Hello!" said the woman, "my name is Sandi. You are going to explore the Clip 'n Climb Centre." "But I don't know how to climb!" "That's why we are here to help!"

by Lina

A Dragon Adventure

Many many years ago there was a war between good and evil. When the war ended the balance between good and evil turned all the good and bad turned to dragons but the war continued.

Chapter 1 - The War Which Is Fake

Now dragons have ruled the world, turned Chelsea Football stadium into a dragon battle stadium.

by Junaid

The Adventure

On a bright morning a girl named Courtney saw presents under the Christmas tree. She had a brother named Ellis, who was cheeky every day. Ellis would go on his PS5. Ellis's PS5 had two controllers[...]. What will happen next?

by Courtney

Once upon a time, two little girls named Nialah and Kenza, they went to Westfield. "Let's go to McDonald's!" said Nialah. "That's a great idea!" exclaimed Kenza. So they went in and ordered their food. But they couldn't go! It was so packed, everyone was screaming. A tarantula on the loose! Dun dun dun.....

by Kenza

Jay and The Murderer

There was once a boy called Jay who got to go to McDonald's. However, he always met a grumpy teenager that was called Ky. One day when it was Jay's 8th birthday and they went to McDonald's but this time the teenager was murdered for some reason. Suddenly they heard a loud bang and Jay and his family hurried out. Jay and Jay's great-grandpa were especially lucky because he was as slow as a tortoise because the wall and ceilings fell down-- CRASH!!! 150 people ended up dead that day and the police got murdered.

THE END.

To Be Continued

by Filipp

♥ Memories and Love in School ♥

I love my school! I'll tell you why, my school is no ordinary school! It's one of the best schools in London! I literally have SO MANY friends. In fact, my whole class is my friend(s). We are amazing together. To be honest, I have more than one BFF, because all of MY friends are loving to meee! Including you! You know I'll tell you about my past generation. So, I lived in a British country and my mum and dad lived in Pakistan and was gonna pick me up from birth, we used to live in Wandsworth and NEVER EVER late to school, NEVER! My attendance WAS ALWAYS 100%. Years later, when I was seven, my mum and dad said we are moving VERY FAR AWAY and move school, I was horrified! LIKE I'M NOW! But the principal Mr Gibbons let me come back! But tomorrow I was delighted and so was my parents and more and more! So, I lived happily ever after forever! I'm done, like it? Still fancy to stay?

It's non-fiction of my life ♥

by Muneefa

One day there lived two girls who went to Clip 'n Climb. Their names were Nialah and Sidra A. So they wanted to climb the walls but Sidra A fell. But luckily Nialah jumped down and saved her. But Nialah was too late. Dun Dun Dun. And a tarantula jumped on Sidra's face. But Nialah was too scared...

by Nialah

I like football. It has a match and I got 4 trophies. I play a match and I scored 13 goals at football. I play striker. My team is Manchester.

by Hamza

Happiness

Walking up Bloemfontein Road, the cool wind keeps pulling me back making my jacket left up in the air like Batman's cape. I keep walking forward. I should speed up because I am late for my sessions.

Will the water be cold today? Oh, whatever! Let me just cannonball into the deep end!

I'm cold! I'm freezing! I need to get out!... Oh, wait… I'm not cold anymore. It's time to have some fun!

All around me the glittering water is pulsing up and down. The children are joyfully splashing as if they were bouncing on a trampoline. Others are jumping about like dolphins diving in the ocean.

"Hey, Mum, look at me!"

It's time to do some flips, handstands and cartwheels. Next, I will glide under all the swimmers. I'm getting better at holding my breath.

15 minutes to go! I'd better do some races and laps with my mum before time runs out.

I love coming to the Janet Adegoke Swimming Centre. I can't wait to come back!

by Angeline

Part Two

These short stories and poems were created during a six week after-school writing group held between SEACC (Sands End Arts & Community Centre) and SEAPIA (Sands End Associated Projects in Action) and a 3-day half-term creative writing camp held at SEACC during the easter holidays.

The authors of these stories range from seven to twelve years old.

The End

A gnome popped out the drain.

"Hello" Miranda said, "is it Poppy, Sage or Ale?"

"Neither" said the gnome, "I'm parched!"

"Oh, hello Parched!" said Mimi.

"No, I am parched," explained the gnome.

"Yes, I know, you told me!" persisted Mimi.

"Can I have some water now?" asked the exasperated gnome.

"Sure Parched!" replied Miranda.

"For the last time, I was parched, then you gave me water, I am no longer parched and my name has always been Petal!" said the gnome.

"Oh," said Mimi, "so sorry!"

She brought Rose into the kitchen and made some tea and biscuits.

"I hope your journey here from Unmatched was alright?" asked Mimi.

"Well, you know they have installed a new entrance on the Golden Gate Bridge so it was much quicker!" exclaimed Petal, "My friend should be here soon."

"Is he parched?" inquired Mimi.

"Yes, how did you know, in fact his whole name is Parched the III!" he squealed.

"Oh" replied Mimi.

by Albane

Marketplace

Piles of passionfruit
Mangoes galore
Handfuls of berries
Want some more?
The whiffs of spices
The feel of cool wind
They lower the prices
as I walk in
I taste a French pastry
Slurp down my peach tea
Find anything the heart desires
at the market of your dreams

by Zoya F

Technology

A tablet, a phone
All what we own
Technology, Technology
Magical if in the past it was shown.

by Sofia R

Dragons Are Real

Many moons ago there was a city in Roma. Roma was very rich but there was one problem. A rich man's home was getting took over by a dragon!

Every night you can hear him snoring from miles away. The rich man had to do something about it so he went to the witch's hut.

When he arrived, he asked for a potion. The witch chose a random one. He turned into a …. Lion. He got back home and waited until night, but the dragon wasn't there. He looked around but no one was there. He waited for the next night and the dragon was there. He ate the dragon and the dragon was defeated.

The END
or is it…?

by Oscar M

"What if a koala went on an adventure?"

A koala sneaks on a plane and waits until it takes off then it starts scratching people and then he goes back to Australia to go back to the trees to climb again and went to go see other koalas in Australia to go see his family.

by Malaika J

The koala took a ticket for the ship and sailed off to an exotic land in the distance. Halfway there he takes a jump in the sea. He shook it off and finally found his way to the land and found its brand-new house full of delicious fresh new leaves to chew on.

by Malia C

It would wear a hat, an adventure suit and exploring glasses. It would go exploring in the forest and have a great, amazing day. The koala will see a spider, slugs, snakes and other creatures. It would sleep on long trees have food when this man comes every day and knows where to go. And travels the world after.

by Cienna D

He will probably go on an airplane. He will probably sleep the whole time but let's see what he is up to. He's eaten and slept, went to the toilet, tried to escape, escaped went to the captain and released all the animals, went to the captain again and the plane crashed.

by Nadia C

What Is a Griffin?

A rustle from the bush
It soon set fire
A flap of its wings
A mean desire.

A screech, two more
Filled the air
Not a wolf, not a bear …
Who what where?

A tail whipped me
My eyes are closed
A fire crackled, so hot, so crispy
It would burn my toast.

I opened my eyes
Panicked and afraid.
A beak, two eyes
I fell back in surprise.

by Sofia R

I Can't Stand!

I can't stand when people talk,
in the library,
there is a sign,
can't they see
BE QUIET IN THE LIBRARY!

I can't stand when people chew
with their mouths open,
to be polite,
there's only a few
SHUT YOUR MOUTH WHEN YOU CHEW!

I can't stand it when someone
when people come in my room,
there is a sign,
can't they read
ENTRY IS FORBIDDEN!

I can't stand when people scream
and throw a tantrum.
You can do that
when you're 3
BE QUIET AND SHUT UP!

It always annoyed me you see,
when people get mad at me!
Stop telling people off they say
WE CAN'T STAND IT TOO!

By Albane

Untitled short story A

In the land of Netherland there was a princess very beautiful but once she put on a mask and never took it off. The people of the town wondered why she didn't take the mask off until she revealed the secret a year later. The whole town was in shock and protested to let the princess go.

The secret was that she wasn't the real princess and the real princess got turned into a frog by the evil witch when the witch saw the news she was worried and hid the frog princess in her basement....

"Uh oh" the witch said the spell on the princess has worn off the people burst in to find the princess.

The witch tried to put a spell on them but seemed to know that didn't work. She knew that she was doomed they got the princess and put the evil witch's house to fire.

by Linda T

Oldilocks

A witch once turned Goldilocks into an old person so her friends called her Oldilocks instead of Goldilocks. It was really hard for her to wake up but she made it home. The three bears were stunned but now baby bear couldn't play with Oldilocks.

After a week Oldilocks was back to Goldilocks so baby bear and Goldilocks can play again. Goldilocks told them what happened and then they told the police. So the witch was sent to prison.

by Nadia C

The Sweet Shop

Gobstoppers, tongue painters, brain lickers
all in old-fashioned glass jars
Chocolate-covered coffee beans, gummy worms
all sold by the old dame
"Come, come and try one!" she hollers.

by Andrea Q

Darkness

No one saw the darkness,
creep in the side of town,
black and purple tendrils,
a silent darkened sound.

It wavered around the edge of town,
and weaved through the trees,
and then it went round the wooden fence,
and into the cricket green.

First the Mayor's house went out,
then the grocery store.
I can't buy my Cocopops,
well, not anymore.

The darkness went on holiday,
and then came back again,
this time it was angry,
and took the swimming pool.

My road went next,
and now I use my light,
it's pink and blue and very nice
I got it at the store.

Now the town is dark,
all of it is dark,
we don't know why,
or when or how.

The darkness comes and goes,
it's strange I guess,
they made a large discovery
it's called day and night!

by Albane

Mysterious Box – Vegetables

A mysterious box appeared in town 2 days ago. Nobody knows what's inside, they can't get it open. Since its arrival half the town has grown vegetables on their heads. This morning, my headteacher came into school with a carrot sprouting out of her head and all the English teachers had broccoli on theirs. Bill had a beetroot on his.

Nobody can prise open the box and stop the curse of overgrown spuds on my aunt's head. Perhaps it's a good thing. I can definitely get used to having cucumbers whenever I'm feeling peckish!

Actually, never mind. I'm only an hour into having cucumbers on my head that I'm really craving something else… Perhaps the parsnips on the mayor's head?

by Alessandra Q

"What if you were able to play your sport for your favourite sports team?"

I like playing football because it's fun and I like the team sport because most of my friends play with me. Also, I got really good at it because in our school we have a football pitch and even though I don't practice a lot in school and playcentre I still love it.

by Cienna D

I would play for Manchester City because that is my favourite football team. I would like to be a midfielder and I would like to win the world cup 3 times and I want to be the GOAT player.

by Ralph B

One sunny day a person called Gracey loved playing hockey. She always watches it on TV. She plays it every day! It's her dream to be a famous hockey player. Her favourite team is Team Wonders. They always win and they work together. When she leaves the house she looks for a person from Team Wonders.

by Oscar M

What if I got to play on my favourite gymnastics team. It would be a dream come true. What if it was on the moon, I could fly high while doing flips but can it become true it would be a dream if I got to play on my favourite gymnastics team on the moon.

by Linda T

Phone

Ringing! My mum is calling.
Ding! My friend's face pops up on the screen.
Pop! My daily news feed has arrived.
Ping! I send a message
half-way around the world

by Alessandra Q

Untitled short story B

There once was a witch that lived alone. One gloomy day the witch said to herself "I need a cat" before long she dashed to her spell room rummaging through her cupboards. Crash! Bang! Boom!

"Finally," she shouted saying the magic words.

"What!" she shouted enraged suddenly an idea popped up in her mind, "yes" she said running to her potion room "this that and this."

Mixing up 4 potions together. "Finally I did it."

The next night she ran to a house in her grey cloak and she kidnapped the child who was asleep. She gave them the drink.

Cliffhanger sorry ☐

by Rosalie A

The Beach

The ice-cream van packed close to us
Mother needs to buy some. She must, she must!
The waves were crashing right on the rocks
Where my friend and I put our little box

A box full of wild flowers.
Some red, some prune.
We will share them
between me and you.

Their scent irresistible
Each better by the next
Our favourite is the red rose
It is better than the rest

We jump in the water
to retrieve our little box
It is not to be found.
Must be lost.

Salt water filled our dry and hungry mouths
Made us thirsty.
But we had to go now
So we went home, sweet and sound.

The gritty sand gave a crunch on our teeth
Exfoliated our feet
The sound of that made me weak
Yucky!

I love the beach
It is the place to be
Can't wait till next week.
We will go again, just you and me.

by Sofia R

Light

The wind and the moon,
together made whole.
I see the cluster,
the crags and the holes.

The light is not scars
not dark but not light.
I see a large owl,
strong and in flight.

I often wonder,
when the people will see
How much beauty,
there is to be seen.

So open your eyes,
let some light in,
and tell yourself,
that beauty is no sin.

By Albane

The Unknown Power

Once many moons ago, there was a young boy called Jake. Jake was playing basketball and he noticed he was bouncing the ball high. He played tennis and hit it miles up in the sky. He now knew his secrets, he had SUPERPOWERS!

He did other tests and they didn't work. Jake went to school and got angered by the bully and fire burst out his mouth. He knew straight away he had more superpowers. He could cook food in less than a minute, but... he could only use it when he is mad. Jake got home and heard his mum say that he is going to a roller coaster ride. He was so cheerful he got outside and jumped around while he was jumping, he started to lift up. He could fly but only when he is excited.

Jake could hit hard normally, breathe out fire when he's angry and fly when he's excited. What's next? Sadness? Worried?

It's up to you ...

by Oscar M

"Lost in a forest"

So, first he arrived in the first forest. Who knew what was in that forest? Maybe an army of Zombies!

He rapidly made his way through the first half of the forest. Where he came to a wide opening. He stopped to have a breath, SUDDENLY! A big large monster popped out. In a deep dark voice, the monster said
"I am known as

by Henry L

My brother and sister went out and played Sunday. They lost their names which were Amber and Richard. They went into the forest they got lost then me and my family looked and they found something that belongs to them so they slept.

"Brother, I want to go home" she mumbled.

"Don't worry."

by Yusra M

Once upon a time there was a brother and sister who were told to get wood for the fire so the brother got the pieces and the sister got a big basket so they went off. The boy Jack cut a tree down and put it on the girl's basket. The girl was called Milly. Milly found money on the floor so she went and grabbed it. The money kept on moving. Milly dropped the basket and ran off Jack was alone but an old woman came and took Jack. After a month the old lady gave Jack some wood and Milly came back home. Jack was lost but he finally got home.

by Nadia C

Me and my big brother went out in the forest to find berries. We then got lost in the forest and it's winter! We tried to find our way back but we got lost even more in the forest!

by Ralph B

Bill and Max were told to go outside and play basketball but their ball gets lost in the forest so they go after it they end up lost and can't find their way back. They know they're going to be long so they looked for food.

"Bill! Max!"

"They're gone" said Bob when they found food but they needed to cook it. It was some spare meat on the ground. They were freezing it was winter! They somehow got a fire. They were warm and they had something to eat.

"Max… Bill. Where are you?" Bob shouted.

Bill and Max saw ice on the floor. Max put it in a bottle. It was water.

"Jack, Bill," said Bob.

by Oscar M

Love

If someone loves you far and near
it will break a mountain.
If love is strong and sound
then no obstacle will bar it.
For if you love and if you're loved
then nothing will stand in your way.

by Albane

Short Story

"And this is how the Egyptians were one of the most impressive civilizations in the whole history of the Earth" concludes my incredibly boring history teacher. It was just another ordinary history lesson until my father burst into the classroom, grabs me by the ear and tells me that we need to leave town in an hour. He then grabs me outside, bundles my brother and I into our old, run-down Audi and drives my family off at top-speed.

After at least 20 minutes of stunned silence, my father announced what this was all really about: at the lab in which he works in, it was prophesised that a monsoon of poisonous, acid rain was going to befall us all very, very soon. After hours, or perhaps even days, we arrived into a very dark and deep forest in which we trekked for hours until, deep underground, there was a small bunker. It had all we needed to survive for the years during the monsoon.

All of a sudden, I heard it. The rain had begun. At first, it was nothing more than a gentle tapping against the roof of the bunker but then it became a stronger, faster tapping which rapidly evolved into a full-blown rainstorm. It raged for many days until we ran out of food. My mother put on a special rain-suit to protect her from the rain. A few days and we took turns until one day, my mother went out and accidently left the door slightly open. The rain streamed in. Using her instincts, she tried to use the sleeve of her raincoat to close it up. However, the concentration of rain was now too potent. She had gotten wet; I never saw my mother again. Life in the bunker then became dismal and dark. Although she had saved our lives hers had gone.

After a few days, we wondered if we would ever feel the warmth of the sun or at least a day without the tapping of the rain. The rain that could end all of humanity.

Months later, we began to notice that the rain was not so loud and strong. We even at times could not hear the rain at all. Slowly, we relaxed and even went out a few times without our rainsuits! However, it was a false alarm. My father had gone out to a meeting with the other survivors when the rain began once again. Perhaps he survived.

Days later, my brother and I discover a toolbox in which you could contact other bunkers. No one reacted or replied to mine or my brother's cries and pleas for help. So, we waited. We got on with our ordinary lives whilst the rain keeps tapping and tapping. I wonder if it will ever stop.

Perhaps it could, sometime in the future. In the meantime, the rain taps on the bunker roof.

by Alessandra Q

The Lone Wolf

Sitting beside this crumbling mountain
The river beside me, made of tears
The great have wealth
The low walks in stealth
The moon shines bright over the animal
In pain, injured, left in vain.

by Sofia R

The Magic Gems

Once upon a time, there were 2 friends Timmy and Isabel. They were talking in the jungle, when Isabel said "I don't feel so good". That's when Isabel's foot turned green! Timmy explained "I'll find the magic gems. I'll bring them back; they will help you." He said. So, he set off to find the gems.

by Henry L

The Moon

The Moon
It orbits us.
It shines and provides a glow in the night,
The moon.
It's our sense of night and day
The stars
They are similar to the moon
They twinkle
The lake
It holds a reflection
A box of some sort
This box holds a key
this box holds the moon

by Zoya F

"What if a monkey escaped the zoo?"

If a monkey escaped the zoo it would jump on cars
and climb on trees. This would be bad because
some people might not like monkeys and maybe be
allergic to them.
It would eat all the fruit and veg and there would
be no more fruit and veg left.

by Cienna D

The monkey might climb on cars and go on
someone's face and climb a house, even release
someone from Prison! It will be chaos.

by Nadia C

It would go back to the wild and take all of his or
her friends with them and jump on cars because it's
a monkey has been in a zoo for a long time it could
be angry towards people and would steal some
food.

by Malaika J

Samurai Ninjas

Introduction

Once upon a time there lived a world of Ninjas until the Snake Master used a spell so powerful, he couldn't control it and Samurai and Ninjas were mixed and now Master Kick is training 3 Samurai Ninja called Bolt, Kia and Tommy. These Samurai Ninjas are going to unleash their full potential and defeat the Time Snake Monster.

Chapter 1 - The Show Off

"Watch this Kia I can control the lights," said Bolt.
"That's just a show off, but this is not" replied Kai.
"If that's not then controlling lights isn't," said Bolt.
"But look at this I can do both" said Tommy.
"That's not fair" said Kai and Bolt.
"Stop showing off and get rest" said Master Kick.

Chapter 2 – No Tomorrow

The next day or should I say, the same day. After a while Kai, Bolt and Tommy realised it was the same day straight away. They knew it was the Time Snake Monster and tracked him down.

Chapter 3 – The Captive Slips Through

As soon as they found him, they took him to the
dungeon. After a while he used a spell and slipped
through the bars.
Where could he have vanished?

by Junaid H

A Poem

The road lays still
The water gently laps

O I wish it wasn't a misery

The land is sparce
The world is quiet

O I wish there was more,
More life …

by Andrea Q

Adventures

I travelled long and far
'Till my legs were like jelly.
At home was my ma
waiting for me with my teddy.

"Come home sweetie!
"Where have you gone"
"Come home sweetie"
"I'll put the kettle on!"

I've ran away
I've gone astray
My ma is waiting
But my dreams, I'll keep chasing.

An adventurer, I am
Travelled the world. What will I see?
Being a slave at home.
Where would I rather be?

Poor ma is home, crying, alone
Lost all hope in me
Should I return? Make her happy?
That decision is up to me.

The wind in my hair
Too nice to share, all belongs to me
I go where I want, when I want
Because I am free

A mythical land, a desert of sand
By me, have all been visited
I want to go where no one went
The island of "Workamisted"

by Sofia R

A Horse and Panda Fight

One day 3 horses escaped from a zoo. They searched for food and water. They came across a group of children. They loved to chase them and they let them ride them. They travelled from London to Manchester. After they stopped for grass.

Soon they saw a panda. The panda was being rude.

Lavender said "stop being rude or I will kick you and chase you until you say sorry!"

No said the panda.

They started an argument.

Then Amber said STOOOOP NOW.

Okay I think that you broke my ear drums. And they all became friends.

Lesson is that you should always be kind.

by Malaika J

Archaeology

Dust and bones,
I'm crazy 'bout,
give me a bone
prehistoric snout!

Some people don't care
but I really do,
some things are hidden,
away from you.

30 odd meters,
under the soil,
bones of mammals,
of knowledge we toil.

Armed with a spade,
and patience all round,
we dig in the soil and
all around.

No bone is too small
no creature too big,
we bring them all back,
in this archaeological dig.

Some people frown,
and say "so uncool"
but I am only happy,
when I'm holding a tool.

by Albane

"What if you combined two of your favourite sports and tried to play it?"

Once upon a time there was a little girl named Lily. Lily liked football and gymnastics so she tried to put them together. Once she did the penguin a handstand and kick the ball to the goal. A second time she did a walking handstand and stuck the ball in its foot. It was tricky at first but she got the hang of it.

by Nadia C

Who would have thought gymnastics underwater. Yes gymnastics underwater its possible hard but possible the most easiest handstand underwater or cartwheel so hard.

by Rosalie A

I would play hockey and football, I would kick the ball and use the hockey stick and the goalkeeper would use their hands and the hockey stick.

by Ralph B

One day I was going to play football so I was exercising by doing a moon-walk with the ball and getting ready. When I was doing the match I did them together it was amazing, everyone was clapping.

by Cienna D

If hockey and climbing at the same time was a sport, they would climb on the wall with one hand. On the other hand, you will hold the stick and try to make it not fall. If the ball got out of the arena it will be a penalty.

by Oscar M

If someone tried to do the combined sports volleyball and gymnastics. You could hit the ball while doing handstands or cartwheels but it could be hard to attempt.

by Linda T

Light Switch

Light is day
Darkness is night
I used to think that at least
Blow out a candle just before I'd sleep
Now things have changed
Now before bed,
I hold a finger to a switch
click
Now I'm asleep
Having good dreams?
I wish.

by Zoya F

Travelling

As I sit on the plane
The dream of flight
soars inside me
The air around me
seems weightless
But at the high
altitudes the
soft clouds
above the emerald
land seem to
change
beyond our imaginations.

by Andrea Q

Poem

A single tree stands on a mountain.
Its gnarled branches interweaving.
Years of strong winds have taken its toll,
the tree slowly bends lower and lower.

Alone on a mountain,
surrounded by stone.
A sprout of life appears,
contrasting to the grey sky.

by Alessandra Q

The Bookshelf

Some give me glares,
Some give me looks,
Some mad as hares
Some so sad, my heart it has shook.

I reached my hand to the prettiest one
But another one called, claimed he is fun.
I looked at their faces
All different, unique.

by Sofia R

Intermission

Miranda was an unnatural baby from the minute she was born. She didn't talk till she was five. On the evening of her fifth birthday, she spoke "this book is incorrect!"

Her parents were astonished and asked why she hadn't spoken sooner.

"There was nothing for me to comment about" she replied.

At five she disproved Einstein's theory.

At six she created a cure for cancer but her parents threw it out thinking it was old milk.

At seven she published a 150-thousand-page book on evolution.

At eight she mastered time, space and quantum physics.

This all continued till she was 13, which is when this story starts.

by Albane

The Cave of Mankind's Secrets

In the ancient times of mankind there was a mysterious cave called Elude cave.... There were many theories stored in an abandoned chest in an unknown place in Elude cave. This was since the beginning of time.

In 400AD, there were 2 boys who lived in Gasalonia who tried to find Elude cave. Their mum was from Hitaly and their dad died of cancer. Their mum would only let them go to the supermarket when she was grocery shopping.

After, the boys paced up and down to think of a plan. They would escape, so they had to pack up orange juice, cheesy toes and a torch. The plan was to bribe the cops to arrest the mother for kidnapping.

As they set on their journey, they glanced at the fragile map. They realised that they had to hire a boat to cross the Pacific Ocean. So, they visited a friend called Thomlan who had lots of boats.

When they got there, they asked how many bitcoins to purchase the mother boat, he said 6 bitcoins. The boys agreed and paid but there's a catch which is that the Pacific Ocean had an unknown species...

In the middle of the Pacific they crashed and then KO'd. When they woke up, they saw the Elude Cave and the chest of many theories that were answered…

They saw many booby traps like poisoned darts and maces. They were SHOCKED!!! But in the meantime, one of the boys was hit by a dart and died. When they made it to the chest the boys died as the other one saw something special inside the chest but the unknown had awoken.

by Thomas M & Nolan M

Project Artists

Tom Mallender

Tom Mallender is a poet and documentarian specializing in the use of archive and found material. When not copying down bits of interesting graffiti, signage or overheard conversation he can be found indulging in many of the vices of a self-proclaimed geek and not writing in the 3rd person.

After graduating from Roehampton University with a specialisation in found poetry Tom gained experience and training volunteering for several years at poetry events ran by Spread the Word and Apples & Snakes. He has been working as a professional writer and workshop facilitator in creative writing and poetry since 2010.

He runs both one day and multipart workshops for all ages and abilities specialising in community emotional wellbeing. This work has been supported using public funding by the Arts Council England via the Grants for the Arts and the National Lottery and seen him working and deliver work with organisations including; Kingston Hospital, Mind, Age UK, Response Community Project, The Royal Star and Garter, SEAPIA (Sands End Associated Projects in Action), Spread the Word, Holy Cross Centre Trust, Gospel Oak Action Link, Iranian Association, Portugal Prints, Claremont Centre, Queen's Crescent Community Association, SEACC (Sands End Arts & Community Centre), It's Not Your Birthday But..., New Unity, and Tate Modern.

Naino Masindet

Naino Masindet is a poet who writes on a variety of subjects through an emotionally informed lens drawing on classical influences. Also influenced by found material, her work lends itself to varying layers of interpretation and emotive depth.

When she's not writing poetry, she enjoys gaming, music, friends and falling into pitfalls of cliché.

Joyce Osei

Joyce is a Diversity, Equity and Inclusion (DEI) consultant, published author and co-author.

From an early age Joyce has been fascinated with storytelling and loved to create and tell her own stories.

As part of tackling under-representation in the DEI arena, Joyce wrote and published her first children's book in 2020 *'The Adventures of Amma and Kwessi in Barbados'*. A children's story inspired by her two children and her Ghanaian and Barbadian heritage.

One of her biggest highlights since becoming an author has been meeting the President of Barbados and in 2023 Joyce travelled to Barbados and delivered workshops to three primary schools, including the one her great-grandmother attended.

Joyce has been a School Governor at a primary school in Essex for 5 years and has created and organised annual events for World Book Day enabling the children to use their creativity and be inspired by authors from diverse backgrounds.

Joyce also loves writing poems, cooking and travelling in her spare time.

Richard Trautmann

London-based illustrator Richard Trautmann has been drawing and teaching manga for over a decade and sells his work at Not My Beautiful House gallery in Kingston-Upon-Thames, as well as at illustration festivals and comic conventions all over the country. He teaches classes for all ages and abilities, as well as working with organisations such as the NHS and various London boroughs to help promote mental wellbeing through drawing, with a focus on inclusivity and accessibility.

Kamapala Chukwuka

Printed in Great Britain
by Amazon

36875784R00066